THE SONGS OF

MEERA

A Selection of Bhakti Verses

Manjul Bajaj

AMARYLLIS

AMARYLLIS

An imprint of Manjul Publishing House Pvt. Ltd.
• C-16, Sector 3, Noida, Uttar Pradesh 201301, India
Website: www.manjulindia.com
Registered Office:
• 2nd Floor, Usha Preet Complex, 42 Malviya Nagar,
Bhopal 462 003 – India
Distribution Centres
Ahmedabad, Bengaluru, Chennai, Hyderabad,
Kochi, Kolkata, Mumbai, Noida, Pune

The Songs of Meera: A Selection of Bhakti Verses by Manjul Bajaj

This paperback edition first published in India in 2025

ISBN 978-93-5543-599-6

Cover Design: Wasim Helal
Illustrations (cover and interior): Anupriya

Printed and bound in India by Repro India Limited

Contents

PREFACE

In the medieval era in Rajasthan, in a time and place in history when high-born women were expected to remain confined inside their homes devoting their lives to domestic pursuits, and on being widowed required as a matter of family honour to commit sati immolating themselves on the funeral pyres of their husbands, the figure of the sixteenth-century Rajput princess Meera, or Mirabai, stands out as a towering anomaly. Meera occupies a pre-eminent position among the Bhakti saints of north India, alongside Kabir, Surdas, Ravidas, Nanak and Tulsidas, the only woman in the list. She is India's best known and most widely sung woman poet. In addition to her native Rajasthani dialects, Meera's songs are sung in Hindi, Gujarati, Brajbhasha, Bhojpuri, Punjabi, Bengali and Oriya.

The Bhakti movement was radical and reformist in its focus, challenging the hierarchy of priests and upper-caste men and their rules and rituals, as also the hegemony of Sanskrit as the language of devotion. It created space for women and lower castes in the folds of religion, encouraged the use of vernacular languages and advocated an intimate, personal connection of love between God and his devotees as against the recitation of mantras and the observation of rituals conducted by the priestly class. But even within this peer group of reformist saints, Meera stands out as a fearless and defiant outlier – a princess by birth and a married woman who claimed Krishna as her divine lover and composed passionate poems of love for her God, singing and dancing in public gatherings, associating with men and women from different castes and from all strata of society.

Meera: Life and Times

Much of what we know about Meera's life is based on her poems and on the early hagiographic literature. While a story can be pieced together through these, the dates of Meera's life are uncertain and a matter of dispute and much controversy amongst scholars. Official Rajput records of her natal and marital families do not carry any specific mention of her – as a woman, especially a childless one, she had no status to be recorded in the annals of the Rathore and Sisodia dynasties to which it is believed she belonged. As a woman saint, she had no formal band of disciples, no institutional inheritors of her tradition, no designated keepers of her legacy. There is little presence of her work in the anthologies and written manuscripts of her time.

Though Meera was most certainly a historic person, history has played fast and loose with her – first, either ignoring her because she was a woman or wilfully suppressing her story because her behaviour was seen as a blot on Rajput honour, and later, when her songs and legend refused to die and only gathered power over the centuries, placing her inside many different histories, all partial and coloured by the values and beliefs of the biographers or historians.

Currently, the most widely prescribed to historical identity for Meera is that she was born in 1498 CE and died in 1546 CE, the daughter of Ratnasingh of Merta, the grand-daughter of Dudaji, the founder of that city and great-granddaughter of Jodhaji, the founder of Jodhpur. Her family were worshippers of Lord Krishna, and as a very young child Meera started to believe she was wed to Lord Krishna. She was subsequently married to Bhojraj, the crown prince and eldest son of Rana Sangha of Mewar. Bhojraj died in battle a few years after the marriage, and Meera refused to commit sati claiming Lord Krishna as her immortal spouse. She was persecuted by her in-laws and brother-in-law Vikramaditya, who became the rana after the death of her father-in-law, Rana Sangha. This life sketch stems from *Miram Bai ka Jivan Charitra* by Munshi Devi Prasad, published in 1898. It is subscribed to by other prominent scholars including Acharya Parashuram Chaturvedi whose compilation *Mirabai ki Padavali* is the standard reference text for Meera's poetry.

An alternate view expounded by Padmavati Shabnam places Meera as the daughter of Dudaji and married to Rana Raymal, the father of Rana Sangha (*Meera Ek Adhayan*, 1950; *Meera: Vyakttitva aur Krititva*, 1973). This theory matches Meera's time to that of Guru Ravidas whose disciple she is believed to have been. This discipleship to the lower-caste guru, Ravidas, is an important item of faith with the subaltern and underprivileged segments of society who kept her poetry and legend alive in the centuries immediately following her death. It also connects

Meera to the Sikh tradition, and as a follower of Ravidas, her poetry found a place in Sikh texts. It also places her as a married woman, rather than a young widow, which corresponds better with the tone of her poems claiming to reject the rana's jewels and adornment – things a widow would not be offered at all.

A third history, drawn from *Prem Abhod,* an early hagiography from Punjab, places Meera as a daughter of Mewar who rejects marriage altogether. She is positioned as a defiant daughter immersed in the worship of Giridhar, the mountain-lifter, composing songs and dancing and singing in the company of his devotees. The rana who attempts to kill her is her own father in this telling. A similar version of the tale is also found in Marathi literature of the seventeenth century.

While the narratives disagree upon whether she was a defiant daughter, a disobedient daughter-in-law, an unyielding wife or a wandering widow, they converge at the point that Meera stood up for her own personal and spiritual freedom against a repressive, patriarchal Rajput society which accorded women little agency and respect. They also underline the fact that Meera was a renowned devotional poet and singer of her times, known across different parts of India during her lifetime.

Meera: The Making of a Legend

While dates and genealogy are a matter of debate, the salient events of Meera's life are common through different versions and are referred to by her in her poetry. More than any other Bhakti poet, Meera's poetry frequently references her life.

From these sources it is clear that she believed herself wed to Lord Krishna from early childhood, denied the claims of her subsequent marriage, and was persecuted for this. Two attempts were made on her life by the rana or king, one by sending her poison which turned to nectar on her lips and the other by sending a snake concealed in a basket of flowers, which turned into a necklace around her neck. As rana is a title exclusive to the rulers of Mewar, we can place her with some certainty as a Rajput princess connected to the Sisodias of Mewar. Whether the rana in question was her father-in-law, her husband, her brother-in-law, or even her own father differs through different tellings.

The hymn to Meera in the *Bhaktamal* by Nabhdas, written around 1600 CE, the earliest source referring to her life, goes like this:

> *Modesty in public, the chains of family life –*
> *Meera shed both for the Lifter of Mountains*

The other significant fact of Meera's life, which emerges from her poetry as well as from the early literature, is that she rejected the social restrictions placed on women and actively chose the company of fellow worshippers. Dancing and singing in temples and streets and leading the life of a wandering minstrel was a key element of her devotional style, activities which would be frowned upon by North Indian society even today. Meera travelled widely, visiting sacred towns and shrines linked to Krishna's life. She is believed to have travelled to Kashi (present-day Varanasi) to seek initiation from her guru, lived in Vrindavan for a period, and finally spent her last years and died in Dwarka in Gujarat, by disappearing, as per legend, into the idol of Krishna in the Ranchhodraiji Temple.

Other elements of her legend focus on how, as an independent woman, Meera negotiated the world of men. One story pits her against Jiv Goswami, a famed Krishna devotee of Vrindavan, who refused to meet her because she was a woman. Meera is reported to have told him that Krishna was the only male in Vrindavan and all devotees would do well to regard themselves as female, after which she was granted an audience. Another story details Meera's calling out of sexual harassment by a male sadhu who insisted she sleep with him as that was Krishna's wish. Meera invited him to her bed, but set up the bed in public, welcoming all devotees to witness the union, thus outing him. Yet another anecdote details Meera's letter to Tulsidas seeking advice regarding family members obstructing her devotion, and his reply to her encouraging her to stand firm in her chosen path. Also popular is a tale which narrates how the Emperor Akbar, accompanied by his legendry court musician Tansen, visited the temple in Dwarka to hear Meera sing.

Meera: Pure or Promiscuous

In her journey through the centuries, the figure of Meera has undergone many transmutations. During her lifetime, she was regarded as a woman of questionable character who brought shame to the illustrious Sisodia clan by refusing the privileges of her high-born status and instead roaming the streets as a mendicant. Meera's own poetry discusses her lost reputation, and her discord with her parents' and in-laws' families. According to Parita Mukta's extensive field study in Rajasthan, Rajput rulers and society disowned Meera and supressed her story (Mukta, 1989). Her bhajans and legend were kept alive by men and women from the subordinate sections of Mewar – the weavers, leather workers, Dangis, Patels, and Jats. They saw in Meera a champion who refused the privileges of birth and chose poverty instead, who fought against the arrogance and oppression of the rulers, and challenged caste biases by choosing Guru Ravidas as her mentor. In the centuries immediately after her death, Meera survived in the folklore, art, and culture of the marginalized populace of Rajasthan and Gujarat as an icon of rebellion.

In the eighteenth century, the story of Meera came to the attention of British colonial scholars and historians. Lieutenant-Colonel James Tod penned a romanticized account of Meera's life as a beautiful princess and pious Krishna devotee, married to Rana Kumbha, in his *Annals and Antiquities of Rajasthan*. A gradual process to reinstate Meera into the official history of the Rajputs began thereafter. The Chittor fort was renovated and reconstructed in the nineteenth century and a temple inside it was said to have been built for Meera by her husband Rana Kumbha, who was supportive of her devotion to Krishna. Later revisions to her history made her an ideal wife to Prince Bhojraj (Rana Kumbha's great-grandson). It was suggested that she became an ardent Krishna devotee only after her husband's early demise in battle. The mantle of the evil rana was passed on to his fifteen-year-old brother, Vikramaditya.

Another major reinstatement of Meera away from her rebellious beginnings and into a saintly ideal of Indian womanhood took place when the Indian national movement adopted her as its emblem of peaceful resistance to British rule. Swami Vivekanand invoked her as a symbol of love for love's sake. Mahatma Gandhi in his speeches and writings spoke of Meera as the chaste and ideal wife who quietly bore torture. Gandhi presented her as a paramount *satyagrahi* who turned her husband into a devotee in the end. Meera's example was invoked to motivate Indians, especially women, to participate in the non-violent resistance to overturn British rule. Meera's bhajans were expunged of the segments challenging marriage and widowhood and Gandhi's Meera was presented as a docile, chaste devotee and model wife as opposed to the earlier people's Meera, a rebel beating the drums of freedom. In the visual arts too, she began to be whitewashed – the image of her clad in widows' white, gently strumming the ektara, overlaying that of the saffron-clad drum-beater dancing and singing with abandon in the leafy boughs of Vrindavan.

Another chapter in Meera's saint-or-sinner saga began in the 1980s. Her work first became accessible to the American public through A.J. Alston's *The Devotional Poems of Mirabai*, an English translation of Parashuram Chaturvedi's *Mirabai ki Padavali*. While Alston's translation followed closely the tone of Chaturvedi's original *padas*, it took the figure of Meera to the world and laid it open to American public imagination and poetic discourse. Subsequent works through the 1980s and 1990s by Robert Bly, Jane Hirschfield, Andrew Scheller, Louise Landes Levi, and other Western poet–translators, recast Meera's poetry in a mystico-erotic idiom, highlighting the spiritual longing and sexual passion in her work to the exclusion of other aspects. An American version of Meera, divested of the Indian cultural context, emerged as a spiritual foremother and exemplar of the sacred feminine espousing a range of causes such as feminism, ecology, and women's empowerment, and making her way into texts on psychology, creativity, philosophy, and metaphysical studies. She continues to exert her influence there, an alternate Meera in a parallel universe.

Also, very influential among scholars has been Parita Mukta's 1994 work, based on extensive fieldwork. It presents a version of Meera as a social and political leader and a voice of the oppressed communities of Rajasthan and Gujarat. The figure of Meera emerges as a warrior against gender discrimination and a challenger of patriarchal norms, the performance of her songs in bhajan *mandalis* an act of resistance by poor women and marginalized men.

Meera in Manuscript

The elusiveness of Meera in history is echoed in the lack of definitive sources of her poetry. John S. Hawley's in-depth search for Meera in manuscript sources reveals that in contrast to her male counterparts, like Surdas, Ravidas, and Kabirdas, there is very little in manuscripts dating before the seventeenth century that can be attributed to Meera. One poem that features in the Kartarpur Pothi of 1604 and another attached to Nabhadas's *Bhaktamal* (written around 1600 CE) are the only two poems that can be dated close to her lifetime. Scholars have found another twenty-two poems which bear her signature from the seventeenth century, of which only six are currently traceable. All other Meera poems as we know them today only started appearing in anthologies in the late nineteenth century and early-to-mid-twentieth century. The Dakor manuscript which surfaced at the Ranchhodraiji Temple in 1946 and purportedly contained handwritten poems by Meera has since been proved a fake on many counts.

Though we regard Meera as a single poet and a historical figure when we speak of the songs of Meera, in truth we do not know how many and which of the 200–400 songs sung in her name in Rajasthani, Brajbhasha, Gujarati, and several other dialects were written by her and how many were later additions by poets who identified closely with her and wrote in her voice, using her signature in the last line.

The first published text of Meera's padas was *Raga Kalpadrum* in Bengal in 1920, followed by a 1927 collection by Naval Kishore Press (Lucknow). For the purpose of today's reader, the oeuvre we identify as Meera's stems principally from Acharya Parashuram Chaturvedi's 1932 *Meera ki Padavali* (revised and updated substantially in 1976) and A.J. Alston's 1980 English translation of the same containing 202 padas in all. Most subsequent anthologies, compilations, and translators draw upon these.

Poetic Style

The songs and bhajans of Meera are composed in padas. *Pada* translates as 'feet', and these are short, rhyming lyrics composed to meter with alternating light and heavy syllables. The form was commonly used by wandering minstrels of the time. Its rhyming nature and repetition of the central refrain makes it easy for listeners to participate, to relate to the main message, and to add stanzas in from their own experiences and understanding.

Most Meera bhajans are associated with and sung in specific ragas. The opening or second line constitutes the refrain, and the last line contains the poet's signature. Meera's signature carries her name in association with that of her God, most commonly occurring as '*Meera ke/re prabhu Giridhar Nagar*'. *Giridhar* or 'mountain-bearer' is the form of Krishna that Meera evokes most often in her poetry. He is the young, handsome cowherd who lifted a mountain and held it over the common people of Braj to protect them from Indra's wrath and from the incessant rains and storms Indra visited upon them. It is interesting to note that Meera worships Krishna in a form that mirrors her own concern with the welfare of the suffering masses.

Many of her songs are vocative in nature, that is, the opening lines are addressed to someone. This varies from addressing Krishna in passionate entreaty or open adoration or as jogi to addressing the rana in a defiant, scornful tone, to addressing other women named (as in mother, sister, or friend) or unnamed as 'ae ri' (a general call to a female fellow sufferer or believer). Meera's poetry also relies heavily on first person references, with many of her poems starting with pronouns for I/my/mine, which can turn disconcertingly and without warning to third person references within the same poem, a style element uniquely hers.

A marked feature of Meera's work is its multi-dialect aspect – it is not restricted to her native Rajasthani dialects like Mewati and Marwari, but thrives in multiple dialects of north and west India, like Brajbhasha, Gujarati and Marathi. One explanation for this is that as she travelled through various parts of the country she reached out to the common people in their own idiom and language. A second explanation is that the original pieces were simultaneously translated by her followers into the dialects of the lands she was travelling through. A third explanation is that Meera's songs were the voice of the protest of women and the lower castes against a patriarchal and repressive rule, and to subvert the control of the ruling classes they were deliberately passed on in many dialects ensuring their survival. In addition to this, given their simplicity and easy-to-sing quality, Meera's songs, more than those of other poets of her time, have been modified by the singers who sang them. They exist in different versions of the same song across many dialects.

Major Themes and Imagery

Meera's poems cover a range of themes, but some subjects and themes recur with greater frequency.

Poems of love for Krishna constitute a major part of her work. She details with much exuberance and openness her love for Krishna, of her eyes falling on him, of being pierced by the arrows and dagger of love. Meera is enraptured by the beauty of her Giridhar's form – his attire, his earrings, the peacock feather in his hair. She is drawn deeply to the mesmerizing sound of his flute and speaks with abandon of their meetings and trysts on the bank of the Jamuna. She speaks of being wed to him, of pleasing him, of being sold to him, and also of having bought him. There is an unmistakable joy, a note of playfulness, and of extreme confidence in her bond of love with Krishna in these poems. While she refers to Krishna most often in his mountain-lifting form, she also refers to him in many other ways, establishing a sense of boundless intimacy between them. He is Shyam (the dark one), Mohan (the attractive one), Nandalal (Nanda's son), chitchor (thief of hearts), Banke Bihari (crooked reveller), piyu or piya (beloved), jogi (renunciate), Natwar (dancing lord), Avinashi (indestructible one). On occasion, she refers to him as Ram. The name is used to imply God rather than the Lord Ram we know as the hero of the Ramayana.

Meera speaks of her love as eternal and existing from time immemorial, a connection with Krishna that extends across lifetimes. She invokes many images from traditional lore to underline the strength of her love bond, such as that between the moon and the partridge, the moth and flame, fish and water. Her poetry is lush with images from the gardens and streets of Vrindavan, with the celebration of the colourful festival of Holi, of trysting on the banks of the Jamuna, and of welcoming the lover to her marital bed. In the Bhakti idiom, the marriage bed is used as a symbol of mystical union, but some translators have chosen a more sensual and erotic interpretation. These interpretations are also valid in their own right as in the Krishna–Radha love poetry tradition, explicit sex was often depicted. In the Bhakti tradition, *kama* or erotic love is considered an accepted route to surrender and sublimation. To quote Pandey and Zide (1965), 'In many schools of Bhakti, *kama* was not forbidden. The true bhakta surrenders everything to God. Sex also becomes meaningful when it is surrendered to Him.'

A second theme recurring through Meera's poetry is of rejecting notions of family and class honour and of defying conventional figures of authority such as the rana (her husband or another male figure of authority in her life), her in-laws, and others seeking to stop her from dancing and singing for her God and associating with holy men, participating in temple gatherings of the devout. Here, she recounts the failed attempts to murder her, declares herself safe in Krishna's protection and dwells on the superiority of her spiritual marriage to Krishna over earthly marriages. She questions society's material values and rejects the privileges of high birth, claiming a life of simplicity for herself.

A third theme in Meera's poetry is of *viraha* or separation from the beloved. On the spiritual path, a union with God once obtained is not guaranteed for ever. The devotee is challenged, forsaken, left rootless and anguished by absence, forced to deepen their practice and to seek more intensely to renew their union. Meera's poems of separation are full of grief and anguish and very moving in their plea to Krishna to return to her. In these poems she again uses traditional imagery drawing upon the seasons to express the tumult of her emotions, the passage of days and nights, the pain of listening to songbirds sing unmindful of her forsaken status, the anguish of a burgeoning spring and playing Holi without her lover, the storminess of the monsoon season, the desires it arouses, of clouds waiting to weep.

Images from nature are an integral part of Meera's poetic style. She frequently draws into service the *chakor* or red-legged partridge, who as per folklore swallows burning coals in its desire to be one with the moon, and the *chatak* bird or pied cuckoo, that awaits the first monsoon rain to quench its thirst.

A fourth theme of her poems are those songs that centre on the subject of prayer, practice and devotion. It is in these that we see her connection with Guru Ravidas and her subscribing to the philosophy of the *sant* school. She urges followers to focus their attention on taking the name of God, of devoting themselves to simplicity and goodness, of rejecting false and worldly values. These poems also allude to the *bhavsagar* or ocean of being and the individual soul as a boat waiting to cross it.

Meera in Popular Culture

My first conscious meeting with the figure of Meera took place between the pages of an *Amar Chitra Katha* comic as a very young child of seven or eight years. It is possible that even before this, her bhajans were part of the radio music that played routinely in our home, but I have no definite recall of this. The pretty, pouting, swooning, backless choli-clad princess of the *Amar Chitra Katha* illustrations won a place in my heart instantly and had stayed there over the passing decades as a warm, fuzzy, romantic memory. So, I felt extremely sheepish when I recently read John S. Hawley's essay on how the Bhakti saints and particularly Meera have been subdued in the pages of the ACK comics and made pliable creatures kowtowing to Indian middle-class values. Meera in particularly was repackaged as a paragon of female virtue, obeying and prioritizing her husband first and foremost and worshipping Krishna as a hobby, as it were. But truly, I don't think the comic version conditioned me to virtuous wifely behaviour, as much as it left me fangirling a beautiful princess turned wandering singer. She was my desi dancing queen.

My second significant encounter with Meera was again literary (rather than religious or musical), and again I was intrigued by the enigmatic heroine of Kiran Nagarkar's *Cuckold*, interpreted for the reader in the bemused voice of the prince she was married to.

Along the way there were many more interactions with Meera in popular culture. Her bhajans sung by Lata Mangeshkar, Vani Jairam, and Anuradha Paudwal floated freely in the air of North India. One did not have to go in search of Meera; she was simply there, something of a recurring earworm, her words and tunes playing in a loop someplace close by. Sometimes, she came with Hema Malini's face from Gulzar's 1979 film, sometimes with the face of the TV series heroine who played her. Later she became known to me in the face and voice of M.S. Subbulakshmi and in classical renditions of her work by singers like Pandit Jasraj and Kishori Amonkar.

Meera's presence in popular culture is so pervasive – with over ten feature films, two full-length television series, enumerable musical albums and many novels and plays based on her character – that to enumerate them here would take many pages. I have simply put down my encounters with her in popular culture and leave it to the readers of this volume to reminisce about their own.

Meera and I

A few years ago, I translated a few bhajans by Meera into English for my pleasure. It began with chancing upon Vani Jairam's '*Bala, main bairaagan hoongi*', which I have included in this volume as the piece titled 'Girl, I want to be an ascetic'. This piece resonated with me at a very deep level, Meera's version of asceticism echoing my own desire to be done with the whole discussion around female dressing and adornment. It is not an outright rejection of expensive clothes, make-up, and jewellery, and a deliberate donning of austerity and a renunciate's garbs. Instead, it's a 'whatever works whenever' attitude, a declaration that as a woman she is detached from the subject of how she looks, her mind is altogether on a different quest – for mystical union, for a direct spiritual experience.

So much work has been done on Meera in the last two centuries and she has been understood, explained, interpreted, translated, and modelled in so many diverse and mutually contradictory ways that as one scholar has rightly remarked, these works tell us less about Meera and more about the writer of the work. This would apply to this writer as well. The aspects of Meera's poetry that enchant me are various. Her open adoration of her Giridhar Gopal, her joyful odes to his beauty, and her desire to beat the drum of love is very refreshing in a cultural milieu where coyness is considered the better part of womanliness; her impatience with social restrictions and notions of family and class honour also appealed greatly to me as did her road songs. Meera delights in travelling, in riding the waves, rolling with the punches, taking the ups and downs of life with a steadfast cheeriness, celebrating life with her *sangat* or community of fellow travellers. For me, the song '*Karna fakiri phir kya jiri*' captures this sentiment with great aplomb. She puts her finger on the choice that a traveller's life poses, of picking freedom and uncertainty over the comforts of an easy but predictable life at home.

The other set of poems that appeal greatly to me are the ones in which she addresses Krishna as jogi, seeing him not only as the youthful and daring Giridhar, or as Madan Mohan, the virile god frolicking with his gopis on the riverbank, but also as the austere adept, the renouncer, the fount of mystical knowledge. And in these poems, she envisages herself as an equal partner, a companion on the path.

Notes on this Translation

I started this project of translating Meera's poetry as something of an ingenue, a complete innocent. I had my eight–nine previously translated poems in my hand, a headful of Meera bhajans I had heard at different times in my life, and a willingness to engage further with her work.

As I began in all seriousness to locate Meera and her corpus, it came as a shock to me that the story of Meera that I regarded as the truth of her life was in fact one of many contested stories and none of these stories could be established with any certainty. Further, that only a few of her poems could authentically be traced back to her, the vast majority would remain the subject of conjecture and debate, written either by her or written by inspired followers in the succeeding centuries.

It took me some time to make my peace with these facts. Eventually my mind did come to rest in this understanding that the sixteenth-century Meera does not have to be an individual poet in our twenty-first-century way for her work to matter. She was a devotee, a singer, a leader of a social movement of protest, and the multitude of voices that have joined her over the centuries are a measure of her success in her chosen calling. This collective entity labelled as Meera in shorthand is our precious legacy.

What came as an even greater surprise perhaps, was the extent of already existing research and engagement with Meera's work. She is the subject of a vast number of books, scholarly treatises and analyses, and translations in many languages. Several translations of her work in English already exist, including those by Hirschfield and Bly, Zide and Pandey, Hawley and Juergensmeyer, Keith Hill, Pritish Nandy, Shama Futehally and V.K. Subramanian.

As I worked on this volume, I returned many times to the question of what I hoped to achieve with my English translation of Meera's work that hadn't been done already and was available to interested readers if they looked for it. The answer I arrived at was simple – that if I felt called to towards this undertaking, I should do it in all sincerity and leave it to readers to decide if it is worthy of their attention or not.

What I have set out to do in this volume is to present her work as I read and heard it. This preface summarizes what we know of her life in an unbiased fashion and discusses the underlying themes of her poems, the salient images and emotions that she plays with, and the main elements of her poetic style. The seventy-five pieces in this volume are chosen such as to be fully representative of her range, drawing on different themes from her poetry and showcasing her various moods, her use of imagery, her philosophical beliefs.

In choosing a sequence to lay out these poems I begin with the eight poems which appear in written manuscripts traceable to the historic Meera as per John S. Hawley. These are followed by her more popular pieces for which I have drawn primarily on bhajan music sources as well as Acharya Chaturvedi's *Padavali* and A.J. Alston's *The Devotional Songs of Meera*. The last poem in this volume is the one believed by folklore to be Meera's last poem written just before she merged with the statue of Ranchhodraiji in Dwarka.

In this volume, as in *The Book of Bullah* (Amaryllis, 2024), the preceding volume in this series, I have gone with the decision not to include the original in various dialects alongside the English translation. I believe that the experience of reading two versions together leads the reader into a place of competing sound and syntax, an experience of mental noise and dissonance. I urge my readers to stay inside these English translations for a while, read this volume in an immersive fashion, and to linger over the beautiful illustrations to create moments of pause and reflection. The title of the original poems is given right below the English title. Interested readers will be able to find many of the songs in written and sung versions on the internet. There is also a Bibliography at the end for those who would like to explore the legend and legacy of Meera in depth.

The translations in this volume draw upon repeated reading and listening to the originals, consulting commentaries in Hindi textbooks on the individual padas, and reading the English translations done by other translators to the extent that I was able to find them. (Some earlier translations are currently out of print.) I am indebted to all of these. I have largely sacrificed the rhyming character of the padas in the interest of lucidity and flow. I have tried to stay true to the cultural context and to keep close, as far as possible, to the original images and words used by Meera without weaving in my own inferences into the poems.

In the end, as I present you this volume, I'd like to quote a saying popular in the folklore of Rajasthan:

Listen, sensible folks, work carries forth one's name and fame
Dwell on Meera – she bore no sons, she had no disciples

Over the past year I dived deep into the songs of Meera and read extensively about her life. I slowly understood what an inspiring figure she has been over the centuries and across the globe and felt the influence she wields till today on the imagination of so many. She continues to be a spokesperson for women's freedom and social justice. I felt truly grateful for having embarked upon this journey of knowing her songs more intimately. I invite you to spend some time with me between the pages of this volume, to join me for a few hours or a few days as I walk you through a selection of her poems in English translation.

.1. The Lotus-Eyed One

मन हमारा बाँधियु कँवल नयन

Mother, my mind is bound
to the lotus-eyed one's attributes
A sharp arrow pierced the body
and went right through
When it struck, I don't know
I'm in unbearable agony
Charms, spells, medicines fail to remove it –
Is there any cure for this excruciating pain?
You are near, not far, rush to me
Meera's lord, mountain-bearer, cool this body's fire
Mother, my mind is entwined
with the lotus-eyed one's attributes

.2. How to Tell True Love

साची प्रीति ही को नाती

What is true love related to?
Ask Vrishbhanu's daughter* –
drenched red in her passion
for Madan Mohan, the erotic charmer
Love's chains are powerful
controlling even an elephant in rut
Meera's lord is the clever mountain-bearer
His palace is a bower.

*Radha

.3. Feverish With Hope

भाय री शायेबा पकरी ज़र् से

The body is feverish with hope
anticipating union with my lover
If not in this world
Hari will be in the next
Nanda's son I will never leave
I will meet him beating my drums
Body-mind-wealth I offer to his youth
Lord, send Murari to me
For her mountain-bearing God
Meera will surrender everything

.4. Listen To My Plea

सुनो यानी घ्यान अर्जी

Listen to my plea attentively
Ram, take me across
if it pleases you
Mother, father, family, heirs –
all are self-serving notions
I'm being swept by the current
in this ocean of being
Take my arm, pull me out
Meera's lord is the courtly mountain-bearer
She is blessed with good fortune

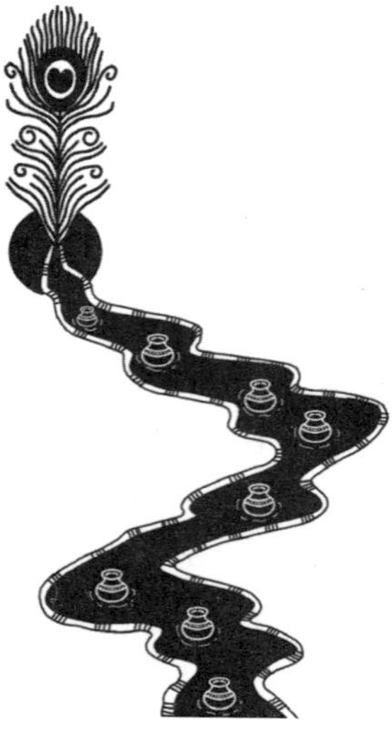

.5. Never Will I Forget Hari

नहीं रे विसास हरी

Never will my soul forget Hari
Never will my inner self forget Hari
Gokul on this side, Mathura on that
The Jamuna flows in between
I wade into the Jamuna waters
bearing a clay pot on my head.
Leaving Radha in her palace
he comes to love this hunchback
In the woods of Vrinda
he herds cows
a flute against his lips
Meera's lord is the courtly mountain-lifter
She lays her consciousness at his lotus feet

.6. How Many Gopis Have Come

काती गोपी आयो

How many cowherd-girls have come, friend,
to join the circle dance?
I have prepared my courtyard
with a fresh coat
of sandalwood, dung and clay, friend.
They have decorated their palms red
with eagerness to meet Hari
They wear dresses of nine colours
and pearls around their necks
Servant Meera will meet Madhav
How many Krishnas, how many flutes
will be there today?

.7. The Eyes Are Greedy

नैना लोभी रे

The eyes are greedy
It is impossible to turn them away
They stare straight ahead
Famished, hungering for more
I stand at my door
waiting for Mohan to pass
I remove my beautiful veil
I dispense with all restraint
Mother-in-law, sister-in-law
reason with me night and day
My restless, greedy eyes don't obey
They belong to another now
Some will say I'm good
Some will say I'm bad

All opinions I raise to my forehead
with due respect
Meera's lord is the courtly mountain-bearer
She is his beloved
Without him, I cannot live.

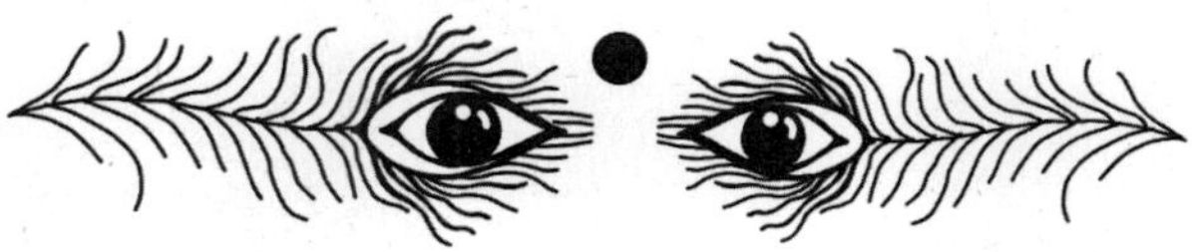

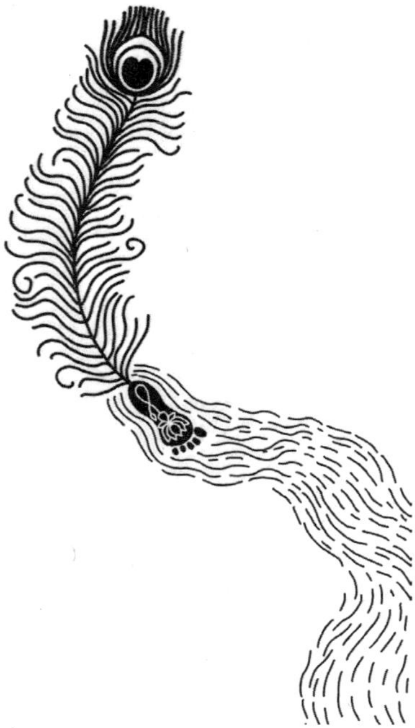

.8. As the Night Falls

निशागत तमचर बोले

As the night falls, someone speaks
Clearing the throat, calling,
'Come to the courtyard!'
Experienced women loosen their tresses
letting the fragrance of flowers spread
Hair cascading down their bodies
like bees hovering around honey
Every limb of the body bears love marks
How can one describe what happens?
Meera's lord, mountain-bearer, owns the night
It belongs to the blue lotus

9. On Seeing Nanda's Son

सांवरो नन्द नन्दन

I have beheld Nanda's son, Mother
All feelings of shame I have lost
My good sense is scattered
The crescent moon shimmers
on his crown of peacock plumes
He wears a dot of saffron
between his beautiful eyes
Crocodile earrings glint against his cheeks
His hair leap in the breeze
like fish dancing on the waves
The Lord has come as a dancer
to beguile the world
Meera is ready to surrender to Giridhar
her every part

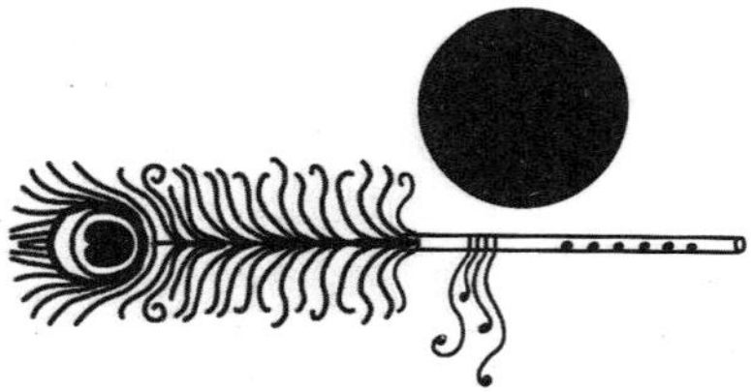

.10. The Sound of the Flute

मुरलिया बाजा जमुना तीर

The sound of the flute
can be heard on the Jamuna bank
It captures my heart
I lose my mind
My lord is dark
Dark his blanket, dark the waters
The music of the flute
scatters my senses
My body grows weak
Meera's lord, mountain-bearer,
Come quickly, take away this pain

.11. Hearing the Flute I Go Crazy

भई हों बाबरी सुनके बांसरी

On hearing the flute, I go crazy
My senses scatter, my heart is enmeshed
What good practices are yours, O flute?
Who is always by your side?
Meera's lord is in the thrall
of your seven notes

.12. Come, Heart, to the Jamuna's Shore

चालो मन गंगा जमुना तीर

Come, heart, let us retreat
to the banks of the Jamuna
The gentle waters of the Ganga–Jamuna
will cool this body's heat

Kanha plays the flute there
and sings with his brother Balbir
Dressed in yellow robes,
a peacock feather in his hair,
diamonds glinting in his earlobes
Kanha plays with Balbir

Meera's lord is the mountain-bearer
No one else but he
Come, heart, to the Ganga–Jamuna's shore
I will bow my head
at his lotus feet

.13. In My Dream I Was Wedded

माई म्हाणो सुपणा मां परण्यां

Mother, last night in my dream
I was wedded
to the Lord of the poor
Fifty-six thousand deities
formed the wedding procession
The bridegroom was Shri Krishna
In my dream, I stood under the wedding canopy
In my dream, Hari claimed my hand
In my dream, I became his wedded wife
Giridhar revealed himself to Meera
She belongs to him from previous births

.14. Mother, I Purchased Govind

माई री! मैं तो लियो गोविंदो मोल

Mother, I bought Hari outright
in the marketplace

Some love him secretly
I declare my love openly
by sounding out the drums

Some call him expensive
Some call him cheap
I know his true worth

Some call him fair
Some call him dark
I know his unique beauty

Some call him heavy

Some call him light
I weighed him on the scale

I surrender my jewels; I take off my armband
I walk the verdant streets of Vrindavan
beating the drums of my love for him

Meera's lord is the mountain-bearer
Her connection to him
is many lifetimes old

.15. I Will Sing Govind's Praise

माई म्हां गोविन्द गुण गास्यां

Mother, I will sing
praises of Govind
I will arise at dawn
head for the temple
and drink the holy water
from washing his feet

Hari's temple will echo
with the sound of ankle bells
as I dance for him
Hari's name is my boat
With it I will cross
this ocean of being

The world is a thicket of thorns
filled with obstacles
Meera's lord is the mountain-lifter
Singing his praises
she will go across

.16. Only Gopal for Me

मेरे तो गिरधर गोपाल

The mountain-lifting Gopal
He is the one for me
No one else but he
He who wears a peacock crown
That is my husband, see
Father, mother, brothers, friends
all I have left behind me
In the company of holy men, I sit
casting aside any modesty
I have left the fold of family
What can anyone do to me?
With my tears I watered
the vine of love
till it blossomed joyously
Meera is your slave, Lord
Let whatever happens happen now

.17. Pierced by an Arrow

आली रे मेरे नैणा बाण पड़ी

O friend,
an arrow pierced my eyes
His sweet form entered my mind
and is settled in my heart
For an age I have stood
at my house, gazing at the road
My life depends on my beloved
He is the life-giving herb
Meera is sold on Giridhar
People say she is ruined

.18. Entranced by His Dancing Form

नैना निपट बंकट छबि अटके

The eyes are struck
by his angular dancing form
They drink in Madan Mohan's beauty, unblinking
Lotus petal brows, fragrant locks
angular pose, slanting flute, turban askew
Meera's lord is so beautiful –
the courtly Giridhar as a dancer

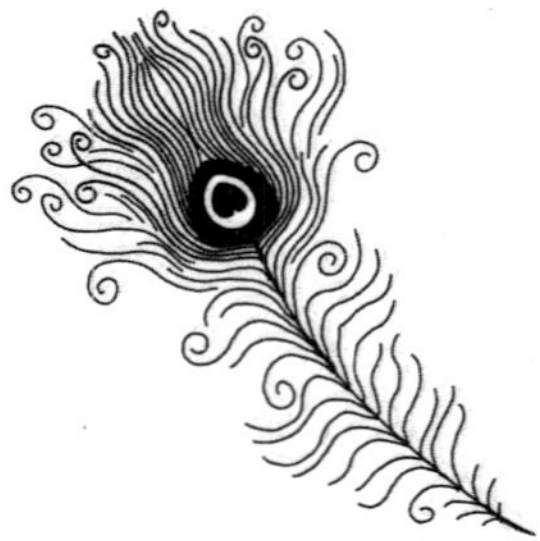

.19. Sister, Kanha Has My Heart

सखी म्हांरो कानूडो कलेजे की कोर

Sister, a piece of my heart
belongs to Kanha –
His peacock crown
his glinting earrings
his yellow dhoti
are so lovely to behold
In the leafy lanes of Vrindavan
Nanda's son dances away
He is Meera's lord
She bows at the lotus feet
of the thief of hearts

.20. Come, Dwell in My Eyes

बसो मोरे नैनन में नंदलाल

Come, dwell in my eyes, Nanda's son
His form is alluring
His visage dark
His eyes so large
Against his lips a melodious flute
In his hair a peacock feather
On his chest a victory garland
On his feet ankle bells
Come, live in my eyes, Nandlal
Meera's lord brings joy to seekers
The cowherd lives
in his followers' hearts

.21. Nanda's Son Captivates

नंदन नंदन मण भायां

Nanda's son captivates my heart
The sky is overcast
Clouds gather, thunder roars,
lightning flashes
The easterly wind blows in
a blanket of dark clouds
Frogs, peacocks, cuckoos –
all make sounds
The blackbird sings a sonnet
Meera's lord is the mountain-bearer
Her consciousness lies
at his lotus feet

.22. Ankle Bells on Her Feet

पग घूँघरू बाँध

Ankle bells on her feet
Meera dances away
She surrenders to Narayana
She is a willing slave

People say
Meera has gone mad
to behave this way

'She is half-crazed,
a blot on our name,'
her in-laws say.

Rana sends her poison
in a cup
Meera drinks it
carefree and gay.

Ankle bells on her feet
Meera dances away
Meera's lord is Gopala,
the mountain-bearer

.23. I Dance for Giridhar

म्हाँ गिरधर आगाँ नाच्याँ री

I dance before Giridhar
I dance, dance, dance away
for the enjoyment of my patron
testing our old love bond
Ankle bells of Shyam's love
I tie, my love tests true
Public shame, family honour –
these I cast aside
The beloved's face is imprinted
on my being
Meera is dyed in Hari's colour

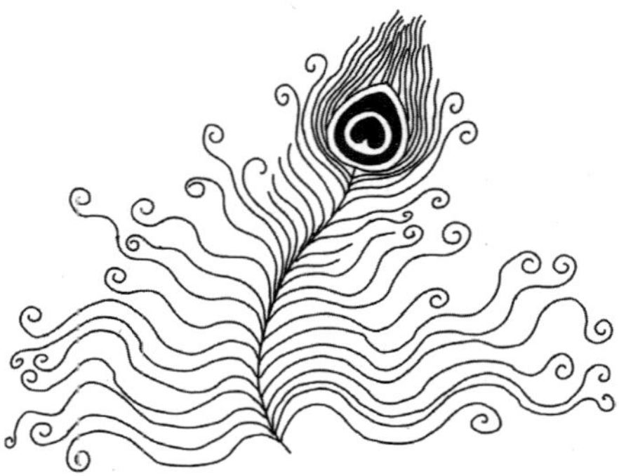

.24. Girl, I Will Be an Ascetic

बाला मैं बैरागण हूंगी

Girl, I will be an ascetic

Whatever guise pleases
my beloved
I am willing to wear –
bright colours or saffron robes
pearls in my hair parting
or hair left hanging loose
My kernel resides with him –
this body is an empty husk
He is my father, mother, family
That is the truth in a nutshell

Girl, I will be an ascetic

.25. I Go to Giridhar's House

मैं गिरधर के घर जाऊँ

I go to Giridhar's house
He is my true love
Seeing him I'm enchanted
As evening falls, I set out
At dawn, I return
Night and day we play
I please him in every way
I wear the clothes he gives
I eat the food he puts out
Our love goes back an age
Without him I cannot live
Where he puts me, I stay
If he sells me, I will be sold away
Meera's lord is the courtly mountain-bearer
She submits to him again and again

.26. Don't Stop Me, Mother

थें मत बरजां माइड़ी

Don't stop me, O Mother
from visiting holy men
Shyam has settled in my heart
No one else pleases me
Everyone sleeps peacefully
My eyes are wide open
Ignorant and deluded is the world
that does not cherish Shyam
He has come into my heart
and now I cannot sleep
Why drink from a pond
that depends on monsoon rains?

My thirst is quenched
with the everlasting fountain
that flows from Hari
My dark beloved is beautiful
I am going to meet him
In separation Meera is desolate
Please accept her as your own

.27. Enough of Big Houses

बड़े घर ताली लागी रे

The grand house I walk out of
locking firmly behind me the door
Good deeds from previous births
account for this fortune
Even great lakes are useless to me
Why would I linger at small ponds?
Ganga and Jamuna I don't need
for I'm headed towards the sea
The company of ordinary worshippers
is not for me
for I follow the Master himself
Petty officials have no hold on me
for I will speak directly in the court
Pewter and glass are not for me
for I wield the iron rod
Gold and silver are no use to me
for I am a trader in diamonds

My star is on the ascendent
The whole mine of gems is mine
Who leaves nectar and drinks brackish water?
Meera's lord is the courtly mountain-bearer
He will fulfil her every wish

.28. If the King Gets Upset

सीसोद्यो रूठयो तो म्हाँरो कांई करलेसी

If the king gets upset,
what can he do to me, Mother?
I will sing Hari's praises.
If the king gets upset,
he can banish me from the kingdom.
If Hari gets upset,
I will wither away, Mother.
I don't care for worldly shame, Mother
Fearless, I will beat my drum
The boat of Shyam's name
will help me cross the ocean of being Mother
Meera seeks refuge in Giridhar
She will cling to his lotus feet

.29. O King

राणा जी अब न रहूंगी तोर हठ की

King, O King!
I am no longer yours to command

I love the company of holy men
I'm through with wearing a veil
Take back your jewels and finery
I'm done with bangles

I have seen my true bridegroom
Palaces and forts
don't please me
I'm done with silk saris

Meera sways enraptured
Her hair hang loose, undone
King, O King!
I am no longer at your command

.30. O King, Why Bear a Grudge

राणा जी, थें क्यांने राखो म्हांसूं बैर

O King, why bear against me a grudge?
Why be as prickly as a desert cactus?

I have left your towers and palaces
I have left your city
I have abandoned make-up
and ornaments
and donned a mendicant's robes

Meera's lord is the mountain-bearer
He has turned the poison
into the nectar of gods

.31. O King, This Loss of Name Is Sweet

राणा जी म्हाँने या बदनामी लागे मीठी

Ranaji, this loss of reputation
feels sweet to me
Some revile me
Some are full of praise
I walk on regardless
upon my contrary path
I meet holy men, hear wisdom
Why would I turn around?
The wicked I don't bother about
Meera's lord is the mountain-bearer
Let the vile burn in their own stoves

.32. Filled With Colour, Filled With Love

रंग भरी राग भरी

Filled with colour, filled with love
steeped in love
I play Holi with Shyam
Colour-filled, love-filled Holi
Gulaal powder rises red
The clouds turn red
My water pistol squirts
sprays of coloured water
fragrant with sandalwood
suffused with saffron
My pot is full
Meera is a servant
of the mountain-bearer
She falls at his feet

.33. The Spring Season Is Short

फागुन के दिन चार

The spring season is short
Come and play Holi

Celestial music fills the air
without a note being struck
The body sings
in all thirty-six ragas

The contentment of my mind
I use as colour
The love in my heart
serves as my water gun

Powder colours fly up
The sky turns red
The colours spread out
without an end

I have removed
all veils from my being
Put aside shame
and fear of public censure

Meera's lord is the mountain-bearer
She lies at his lotus feet

.34. My Dark Beloved Resides in Braj

म्हारो साँवरो ब्रजवासी

My dark beloved resides in Braj
Friends, worldly marriages are false
They are wiped out without a trace
I have chosen as my groom
Hari, the indestructible
The serpent of time cannot take him
My beloved dwells in my heart –
a source of everlasting joy
Meera's indestructible lord,
grant her refuge at your feet

.35. O, Vrindavan Is So Appealing

आली म्हांने लागे वृन्दावन नीको

O, Vrindavan is so appealing
In every house a tulsi plant
In every home Govind is worshipped
The pure waters of the Jamuna flow by
Milk and curds are consumed aplenty
On his gem-studded throne, the Lord sits
wearing a crown of tulsi leaves
From bower to bower worshippers go
listening to the flute's music
Meera's lord is the mountain-bearer
Without worship life is tasteless

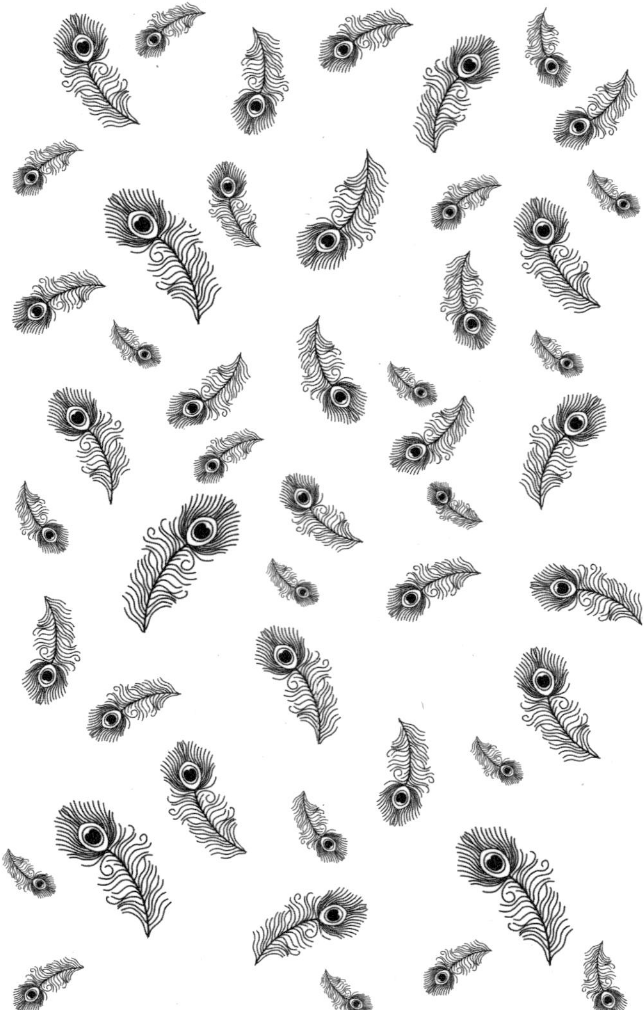

.36. Dyed in the Beloved's Colours

मैं तो सांवरे के रंग राची

I am dyed
in my beloved's colour
Dressed in finery
I put on ankle bells
I shed all shame
and dance
The doubts are gone
I keep the company
of holy men
My devotion is untainted
Every day I sing Hari's praises
safe from the black snake
Without him the world
is a desert
and nothing has meaning
Meera is mad about Giridhari,
glad to be known
as his besotted devotee

.37. Dyed in Giridhar's Colours

म्हां गिरधर रंग राती

I'm dyed in Giridhar's colours
He is my beloved
Dressed in my robe of five elements, Sister
I played hide and seek with him
When he caught me I surrendered body and soul
Those whose beloveds are abroad
write letter after letter
My beloved dwells in my heart
He neither comes nor goes
Meera's lord is the mountain-bearer
She sees him by day and night

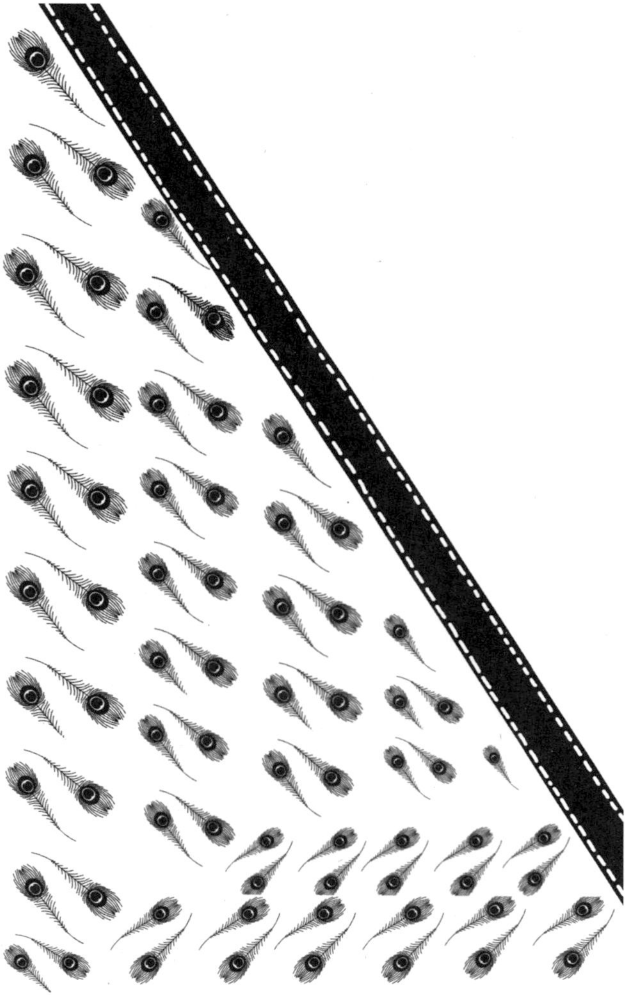

.38. Meera Is Dyed in Hari's Hues

मीरां लागो रंग हरी

Meera is dyed in Hari's hues
No other colour will take
My prayer beads and my tilak
are my ornaments
My good nature my only jewel
No other embellishments are necessary
Thus said my guru
Regardless of blame or praise
I will sing paeans of Govind
The path he shows
is the path I take
I do not steal or harm anyone
What can anyone object to?
I won't get off an elephant
to ride on a donkey
Don't ask it of me

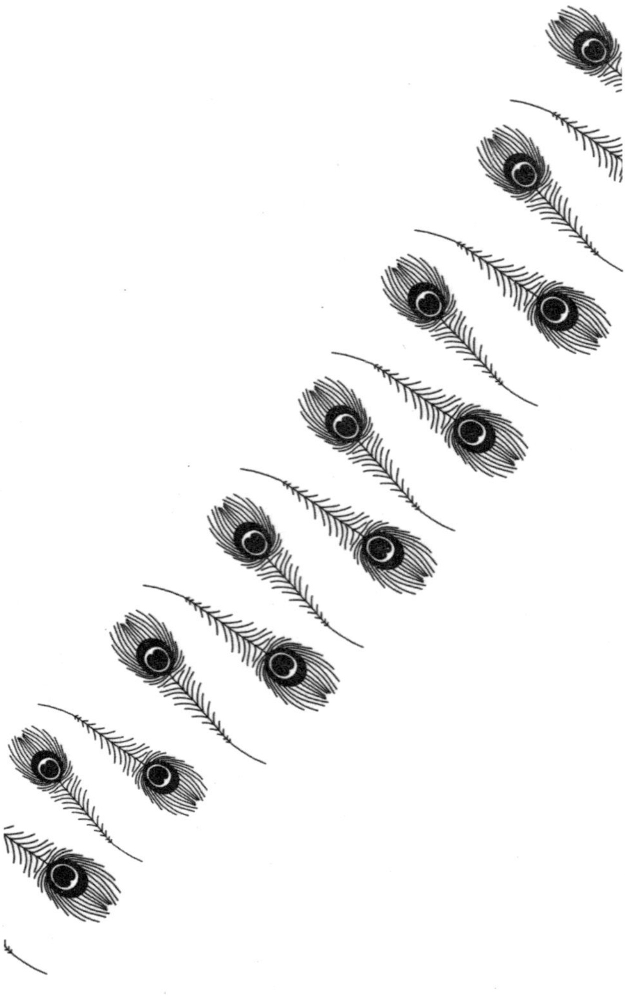

.39. This Dye Is Fast

या तो रंग धत्ता लग्यो

This dye is very deep, Mother
I drank from the cup and began spinning
It is impossible to be sober now
no matter how hard I try
A snake in a basket the king sent
The girl from Merta donned it like a nine-gem necklace
The king sent a cup of poison
The princess of Merta drank it like holy water
She laughed and sang praises of Hari
Now that I have drunk the nectar of his name
no other colour will take
Meera's lord is the courtly mountain-bearer
No cheap dye that will bleed

.40. Cloud, O Cloud!

बादला रे थें जल भर्या आज्यो

Cloud, O Cloud!
You come laden with rain
Tiny droplets begin to fall
The koel sings its song
O Cloud!
Thunder and wind make sweet music
The sky is overcast

Let me spread out my bed
My lover is coming home
Together, we will sing songs
to greet him
Meera's lord is the indestructible Hari
Lucky are those who find him

.41. Make Me Your Servant

म्हाणो चाकर ऱाखां जी

Keep me as your servant, Giridhari
Keep me as your servant please

I will keep a garden for you
My day starting with a glimpse
of you
I will sing your praises
through the leafy lanes of Vrindavan
Seeing you will be my reward
Remembering you my wages

I have yearned for you
birth after birth
wearer of the peacock crown
and ochre robes
your throat bejewelled
Cowherd of Vrindavan

Mohan, the flute-bearer
For you I will make fresh garlands
For you I will don a scarlet sari

My heart is pining, meet me at midnight
Meet me at midnight by the Jamuna shore

.42. What Words Should I Say

थाँणो काँई बोल सुणावा

What should I say?
What can I say?
O, my beloved!
O, my beloved Giridhari
My lover from lifetimes
One look at your beauty
and I was smitten

Come into my courtyard
Women sing songs of welcome
The square is washed
with my tears
I offer to you my body and soul
At your feet I prostrate
For your sake
Meera is still a virgin

What should I say?
What can I say?
O, my beloved!
O my beloved Giridhari

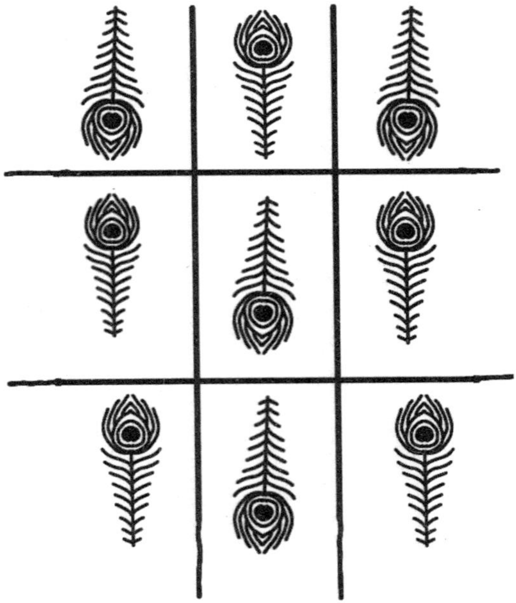

.43. Come to My House, Beloved

म्हारे घर आओ प्रीतम प्यारा

Come to my house, dear beloved
My body-mind-wealth I will proffer
and sit in your worship
You are an ocean of virtues
I am full of flaws
I have no goodness to commend me
but you are forgiveness itself
Meera says, Lord, when will you meet me?
My eyes ache waiting for you

.44. Come to My Home, God

म्हारे आजोय जी रामाँ

Come to my home, Ram
Your coming will bring peace
Meeting you will give me joy
fulfil all my heart's desires
Between us there is little difference
as between sun and sunshine
Meera's heart longs for nothing more –
just her beautiful Shyam

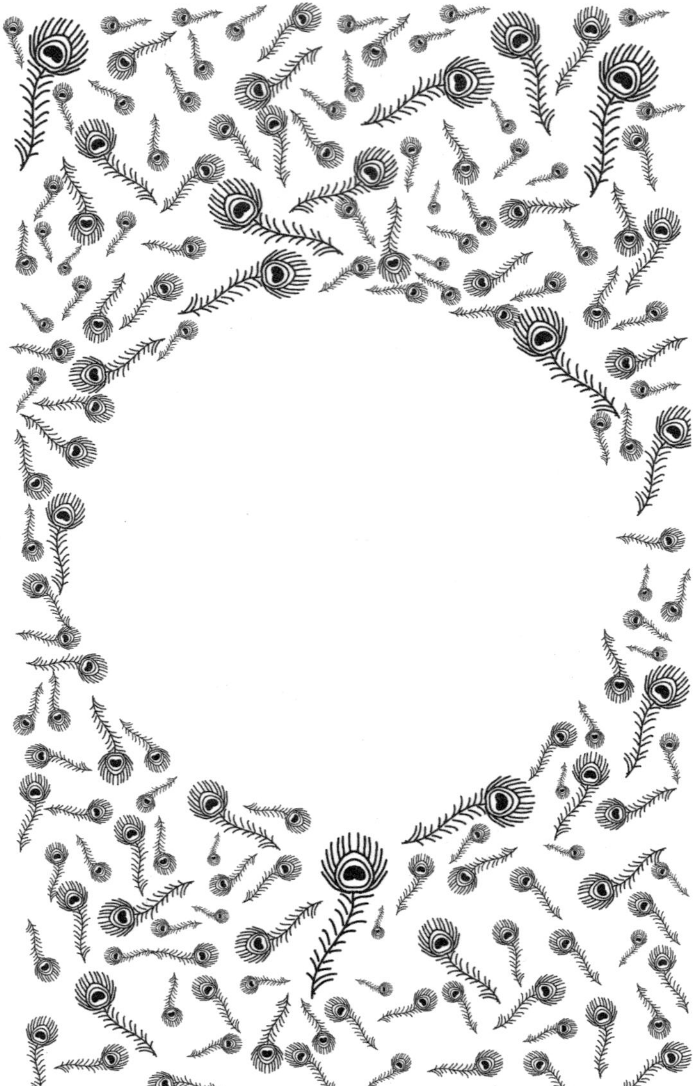

.45. Come to My Place, Lord

म्हारे डेरे आज्यो जी महाराज

Come to my place, Lord
I have picked buds and blossoms
and spread them on the bed
I sit adorned from head to toe
I have served you over lifetimes
You are my bridegroom
Meera's lord Hari, the indestructible
Come, don't disappoint me today

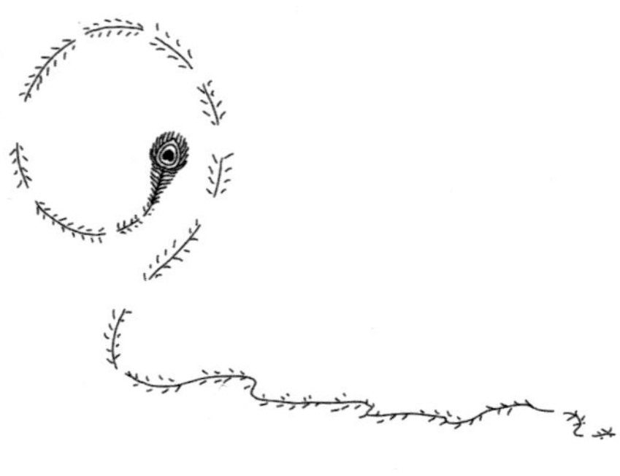

.46. Without the Beloved

प्रिया बिण रह्यां न जायां

Without the beloved
my world is lonesome
Is there anyone
who will take me to him?
I offer body and soul
For you I wander the forests
dressed as a renunciate
Ages have passed, you haven't come
Day after day I wait,
eyes full of longing, tears pouring
Meera's lord, when will we meet?
When will you hold me close?

.47. Friend, When Will I Meet My Love

सजनी कब मिलस्याँ पिय म्हाराँ

Friend, when will I meet my love?
My eyes are fixed on the joy
of seeing his lotus feet
Deep is my desire
to see your face
Despairing, impatient, in pain
Meera's lord, mountain-bearer,
without you I'm in agony

.48. The Eyes Thirst to See Him

अखयाँ तरसा दरसण प्यासी

The eyes thirst to see him
The days pass somehow, friend
The nights are unbearable
The cuckoo calls on the branch
Grief pierces through me
People speak harsh words
and make fun of me
Meera is sold to Hari
His slave, life after life

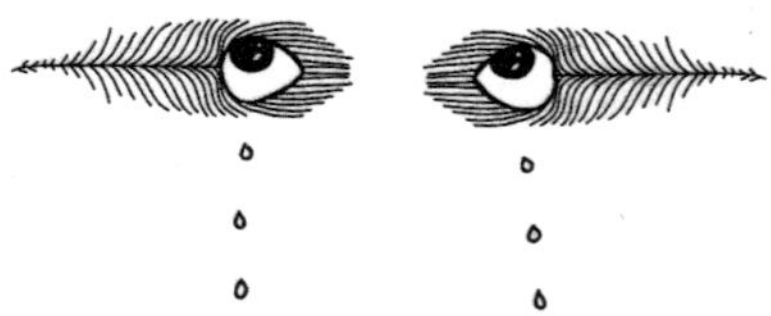

.49. Looking at Clouds I Weep

बादल देखाँ झरी

Looking at the clouds, Shyam
I weep copiously

Dark and light clouds gather
Hour after hour it rains
Everywhere I look there is water
The thirsty earth turns green

Looking at the clouds, Shyam
I weep copiously

My beloved lives abroad
At the door I stand drenched
Meera's lord is the indestructible Hari
May his love be true

.50. With Whom Should I Play Holi

किण सँग खेलूँ होली

With whom should I play Holi?
My beloved has forsaken me
Abandoning jewels and pearls
I have donned tulsi beads
Feasts and palaces hold no charm
For my beloved I'm lovelorn

Why this distance?
If you loved another,
why did you court me?
Ages have passed
he hasn't come
Without Shyam the heart wilts
like an untended vine

Lord, come to Meera
Through lifetimes she has worshipped you
She stands forsaken and lonely

.51. O Singing Bird

पपइया रे

O singing bird
Don't call *piyu-piyu*
so plaintively

Separated from my love
I will take offence
Twist your wing
Cut your beak
Put salt on your wounds
The lover is mine, I am his
Who are you to call out
to him?

But should I meet him again
Your voice will begin
to sound sweet
to me

I will gild your beak
Declare you a favourite
I will write a letter to the beloved
O bird, take it to him

Tell him that
pining for him I no longer eat
Your servant Meera
is in distress
Master of the inner realms,
without you
she cannot survive

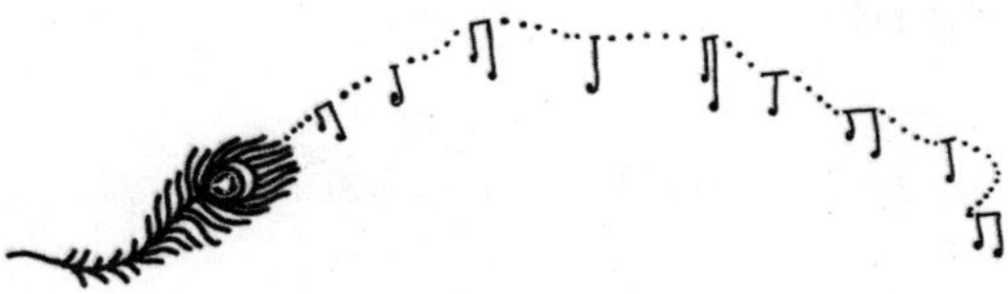

.52. Holi Without My Beloved

होली पिया बिन लागाँ री खारी

Without the beloved Holi is bitter
Deserted the village, deserted the countryside
deserted the bed and loft
Left by my beloved I wander alone
Destroyed by separation
Where in the world can I go searching for him?
The lines on my fingers blur with counting days
Murari hasn't come
Drums, tambourines, flutes play music
The ektara sounds out
Spring is here, the beloved is not
Shyam, I'm in pain
I plead with you, Giridhar, preserve my honour
For you, age after age I have stayed a virgin
Come, meet me, Madhav
In you Meera seeks refuge

.53. Mother, Hari Doesn't Listen

माई म्हारी हरिहूँ न बूझयाँ बात

Mother, Hari doesn't listen
Why doesn't the breath
leave this body now?
He doesn't lift my veil
He doesn't speak to me
The evening turns to dawn
Ages pass without conversation
How am I to survive?
The rainy season, they say,
is the season of Hari's coming
Through the deep dark nights
with flashes of lightning
I count the hours to dawn
Meera is dyed in Hari's colours
In longing her life passes on

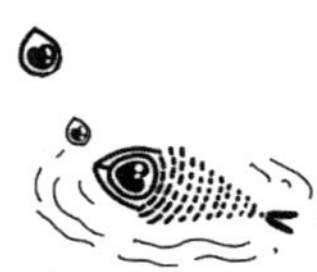

54. Sister, My Sleep Is Ruined

सखी, मेरी नींद नसानी हो

Sister, my sleep is ruined
Awake I watch the path for him
Friends lecture and console
It's to no avail, I don't listen
Unable to see him I'm restless
The body becomes listless
On my lips his name
No one understands
the pain of separation
Like the partridge yearns
for the moon
Like a fish needs water
Meera is bereft, disconsolate
losing all her senses

.55. Love, Ask How I Am

सजन सुध ज्यूँ जाणे त्यूँ लीजे

Love, ask how I am
There is none other for me
Accept me as your own
By day I cannot eat
At night I do not sleep
I am wasting away
Meera's lord is the mountain-bearer
Having come to her once,
do not forsake her now

.56. Beloved, Be True to Me

सांवरा म्हारी प्रीत निभाज्यो जी

Beloved, be true to me
You are the ocean of goodness
I am a flawed being
I care not
for the world's homilies
Speak sweet words to me
I have served you
over lifetimes
Come to my courtyard, please
Meera's lord, courtly mountain-lifter,
Take her raft across the sea

.57. Listen, the Dark One's Gaze

आली सांवरे की दृष्टि

Listen girl, the dark one's gaze is a dagger
Pierced by it I'm restless, in a daze
Pain spreads through the body
The mind is intoxicated
My companions too are in this state
I know him well –
the wanderer of the woods.
The partridge longs for the moon
The moth is singed by the flame
The fish dies without water
Precious indeed is love
Without seeing him, how am I to live?
Go, tell him Meera is his

.58. Don't Speak of Love, O Innocent

लगन का नाँव न लीजे री भोली

Let's not talk of love, innocent girl
The path of love is strange
Step on it and you're wasted
If still you wish to love,
be prepared to proffer your head
In love the moth circles the flame
till it is burnt to death
In love the deer hears the horn
and walks towards the hunter
In love the partridge swallows coals
in its longing for the moon
In love fishes give up their life
when parted from water
In love the bee enters the flower
and lets the petals close
Meera says, My Lord, mountain-bearer
my consciousness seeks your lotus feet

.59. I Am Crazed by Love

हे री मैं तो प्रेम दिवानी

I am crazed by love
No one understands my pain

I wander in the wilderness
No doctor can I find
I know no prayers, no rituals
My eyes are lit lamps

Only the wounded can understand
the pace of a wounded man
Only the jeweller can know
the value of his lost gem

I am crazed by love
No one understands my pain

My bed is on a crucifix
How then can I sleep?
My lover resides in heaven
How then can we meet?

In pain I roam the wilderness
No doctor can I find
If the lover comes as a doctor
this pain will be washed away

I am crazed by love
No one understands my pain

.60. You Can Break It Off

जो तुम तोड़ो

You can break it off
It's not possible for me
Forsaking you, Krishna,
where will I go?
You are the tree
I am a leaf
You are the lake
I am a fish
You are the mountain
I am its spur
You are the moon
I the partridge that longs for it
You can break it off
It's not possible for me
You are the pearl
I am the string
You are the gold

I am its auspiciousness
Meera says, dweller of Braj,
You are the master
I the slave
Forsaking you, Krishna,
where will I go?

.61. Jogi, Come to My Country

जोगिया जी आज्यो जी इण देस

O Jogi, come to this country
Let my eyes behold you
This is my plea
The rainy season is here
The rivers, lakes, land are brimming
What keeps you away?
This separation torments

The rainy season has passed
but my eyes weep unchecked
Just this once, turn around
and come to our town
I cannot forget the idol
that lives in my heart
There is no one for Meera, only you
Come visit me

.62. Day After Day I Wait, Jogi

जोगिया जी निसदिन जोऊँ बाट

O Jogi, day after day,
I watch the road for you
My feet fear the difficult path

The jogi came to my city
Getting no love from me,
he went away
In my innocence I failed
to bewitch him
It's been an age since he left
No signs of his return

Come, end this separation
My body burns
Either he is not in this world

or he has forgotten me
What should I do? Where do I go?
My eyes are useless with tears
The yearning for you fills me

Come, take me as your own
Without you Meera is helpless, abandoned,
her being in torment

.63. Tell the Jogi This

जोगिया ने कहज्यो जी

Take my message to the Jogi, friend
The wise one who meditates
on Shiv and the primordial snake
Tell him this –
I will follow him
Without the beloved this land is strange
Guide me, dear protecter
to where you live
I will don beads and tattered robes
I will take a begging bowl in hand
become a jogini, search the world
walking by your side

Girl, he promised he would return
with the monsoon rain
It has been an age
The lines on my fingers dim

counting the days
My face is sallow, my youth
wears the pallor of age
Servant Meera worships Ram
offers body and mind to him

.64. Loving a Jogi Brings Pain

जोगियारी प्रीतड़ी है दुखडा रो मूल

Loving a jogi
is the root of pain
In your presence
he's all sweet words
Then he's gone
and you are forgotten
Breaking ties is easy for him
like plucking a flower
Meera says, on not seeing you
my heart is pierced by thorns

.65. Grief Comes with Loving a Jogi

जोगिया से प्रीति कियां दुख होई

To love a jogi
is to invite pain
Love has brought me no joy, Sister
A jogi is no one's friend.
I will know no rest by night or day
till I meet him again
In all this world
nothing can match the beauty
of his face
Meera's lord, when will we meet?
When will I be filled with joy?

.66. Let the Jogi Go

जावादे जावादे जोगी

Let him go! Let him go!
The jogi is no one's friend
Sadness fills me
He speaks sweetly
but will not commit
I thought he would take me across
but he left me midstream
Meera's lord is the beautiful Shyam
She loves him despite everything

.67. Remember Me Some Day

कोई दिन याद करो

Remember me someday,
my wandering Lord God
I sit cross-legged in prayer
in the way of devotion
I thought you would take me across
You left midstream
No one sees a jogi come
No one sees him go
A jogi is no one's friend
Meera's lord, O mountain bearing Gopal,
her consciousness seeks your feet

.68. In My Wandering Life

करना फकीरी फिर क्या दिलगिरी

In my wandering life
there is no place for sadness
I remain in bliss

Some days there is a carriage
Some days there are mansions
Some days living in the jungle
it is

Some days on an elephant
Some days on horseback
Some days on foot
I walk

Some days bring a feast
with many sweet treats
Some days I go hungry
without food

Some days bring bolsters
and comfortable beds
Some days on the floor
I sleep

Meera says,
O Lord, courtly mountain-lifter
willingly I endure
whatever comes my way

.69. Seekers, Strange Are the Workings of Fate

करम की गति न्यारी न्यारी संतो

Seekers! The workings of fate
are uniquely strange

The doe has large eyes
but wanders lost in the woods

The tall white crane has a raucous cry
The little black koel sings melodiously

There is sweet water in a spring
The vast oceans are salty

The foolish are rulers
The wise beg on streets

Meera's lord is Gopala
Who cares for the king?

.70. Life Is Short

जगमाँ जीवणा थोड़ा

Life is short
Don't get caught in worldly pursuits
Our parents give us birth
but we are here to serve the Lord
Forget earning and spending
Focus on good deeds
Meera will sing Hari's praises
She cares for nothing else
Meera's lord is the mountain-bearer
He will take her across

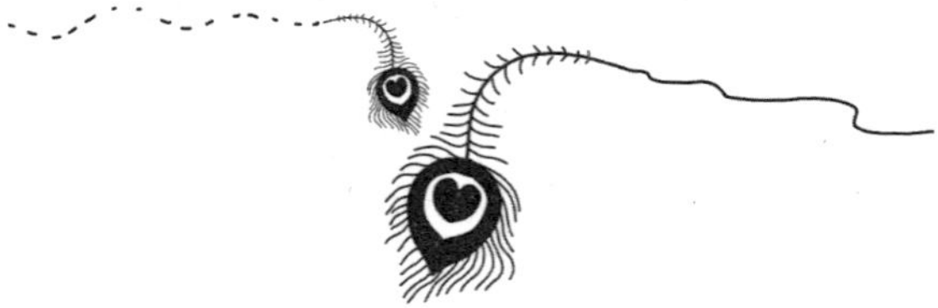

.71. My Mind Repeats His Name

मेरो मन राम हि राम रटै

O mind!
Take God's name again and again
O living creatures!
Centuries of sin are pardoned
by repeating his name
Sins of former lives
are forgiven by chanting
the Lord's name
The name is a draft of nectar
in a golden cup
Who can refuse to take it?
Meera's lord is the indestructible Hari
Her body and mind
dissolve into his

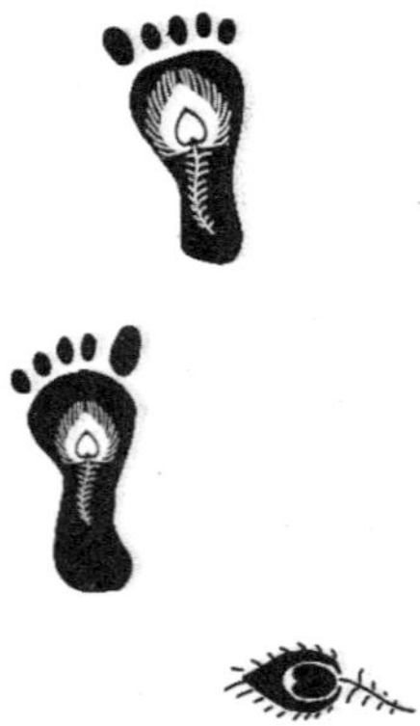

.72. O Mind, Dwell On the Indestructible

भूज मन चरन कँवल अविनासी

Worship, O heart,
at the lotus feet
of the indestructible one
Whatever is visible between earth and sky
will all pass into nothing
Why go on fasts and pilgrimages?
Why turn towards Kashi?
Take no pride in this body
It will be dust one day
This world is the sport of sparrows
It ends when evening falls
What comes of donning ochre robes?
What comes of renouncing home?
Being a jogi is no guarantee
for knowing the secret of liberation
Meera's lord is the courtly mountain-bearer
She asks him to free her
from the cycle of birth and rebirth

.73. Let's Head to That Other Place

चालो अगमके देस

Let's go to that other world
Where Time holds no sway
Where the swan of life
plays in the fountains of love
Where holy men abound
and enlightenment can be found
by meditating on Shyam's name
There, I will don the anklets
of my good deeds
And dance the dance
of inner bliss
I will wear a gold head piece
and bangles of gold
Everything will be for love of him
Nothing else will signify

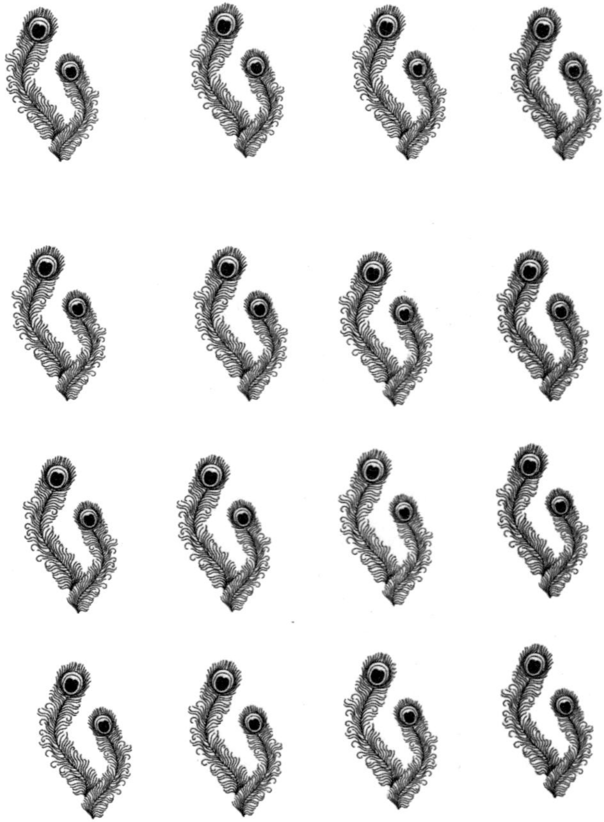

74. Look Towards Me, Lord

थें तो पलक उघाडो दीनानाथ

Look towards me, Lord of the poor
I have been standing a long while
ready to serve
My relatives have become enemies
No one likes me any more
Other than you I have no one
My boat is stuck mid-sea
By day no rest, by night no sleep
I waste away in waiting
Pierced by separation
Not for a moment do I forget you
You rescued Ahalya in the woods
when you found her turned to stone
What weight then can Meera be
compared to that?

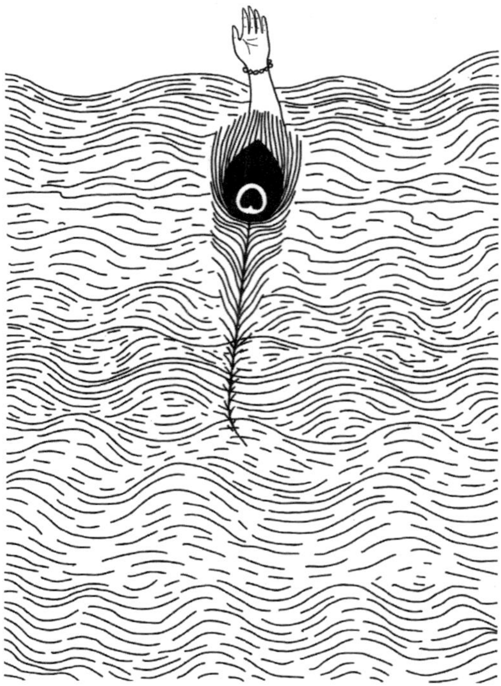

.75. Harī, Save Us from Paīn

हरि तुम हरो जन की भीर

Hari, you alleviate everyone's suffering
You saved Draupadi's honour
by endlessly extending her sari
For your devotee Prahlad you became a man–lion
killing Hiranyakashipu without delay
You saved the drowning elephant
by draining the river
Meera is the servant of the courtly mountain-bearer
Remove my afflictions, please

Bibliography

Historical Texts Cited

Nabhadas. *Śrī Bhaktamāl*. Hariprasad Bhagirath. Bombay

Priyadas. *Bhaktirasabodhini*. Hariprasad Bhagirath. Bombay

Prem Abodh Pothī. Patiala: Punjabi University Publication Bureau, 1989.

Krishnananda Vyasadeva, *Sangita Raga-Kalpadruma Encyclopedia of Indian Music*

Books

Alston, A.J. *The Devotional Poems of Mirabai*. Delhi: Motilal Banarsidass, 1980.

Bly, Robert, and Jane Hirshfield. *Mirabai: Ecstatic Poems* (Afterword by John Stratton Hawley). Boston: Beacon Press, 2005.

Chaturvedi, Parashuram. *Mirabai ki Padavali*. Allahabad: Hindi Sahitya Sammelan, 1973 (1932).

Futehally, Shama. *In the Dark of the Heart: Songs of Meera*. Harper Collins; San Francisco 1994.

Hawley, J.S. *Three Bhakti Voices: Mira, Surdas and Kabir in Their Times and Ours*. Delhi: Oxford University Press, 2005.

Hawley, J.S., and Mark Juergensmeyer. *Songs of the Saints of India*. Delhi: Oxford University Press, 2004 (2nd revised edition).

Hill, Keith. *I Cannot Live Without You: Selected Poems of Mirabai and Kabir*. Attar Books. 2021.

Levi, Louise Landes. *Sweet on My Lips: The Love Poems of Mirabai*. Cool Grove Press. New York, 1997.

Nabhadas. *Srī Bhaktamāl, with the Bhaktirasabodhinī Commentary of Priyādās*, edited by Bhagavan Prasad Rupakala. Lucknow: Tejkumar Press, 1961. (originally 1910).

Nagarkar, Kiran. *Cuckold*. Harpercollins. 2003.

Nandy, Pritish. *Songs of Mirabai with drawings by Rabin Mondal*. Vikas Publishing. New Delhi, 1975

Martin, Nancy. *Mirabai: The Making of a Saint*. Oxford University Press, 2023.

Mukta, P. *Upholding the Common Life: The Community of Mira*. Delhi: Oxford University Press, 1994.

Schelling, Andrew (Trans.). *For Love of the Dark One: Songs of Mirabai*, pp. 147–55.: Shambhala Press. Boston 1993.

Shabnam, Padmavati. *Meeran, Ek Adhyan*, Edition number : 001 Lok Sevak Prakashan, Banaras, 1950 – *Meera: Vyakttitva aur Krititva*, Banaras 1973.

Subramanian, V.K. *Mystic Songs of Meera*. Hind Pocket Books, 2010.

Tod, J. *Annals and Antiquities of Rajasthan or The Central and Western Rajput States of India*. Ed. William Crooke. Oxford University Press. Edinburgh. 1920.

Research Papers and Articles

Bhatnagar, Rashmi, Dube, Renu, and Reena Dube. 'Meera's Medieval Lyric Poetry in Postcolonial India: The Rhetoric of Women's Writing in Dialect as a Secular Practice of Subaltern Coauthorship and Dissent. *Boundary 2* 31, no. 3 (2004), Duke University Press.

Hawley, John Stratton & Mann, Gurinder Singh. Mirabai in the Pothi Prem Ambodh. Journal of Punjab Studies - Volume 15, 2008, pp. 199–225.

Kishwar, Madhu, and Ruth Vanita. 'Poison to Nectar: The Life and Work of Mirabai'. *Manushi* 50–52, pp. 75–92 (1989).

———. 'Modern Versions of Mira'. *Manushi* 50–52, pp. 100–101(1989).

Melnikova, Nora. 'Mirabai – A Saint or a Rebel?' *Cracow Indological Studies* XX, no. 2 (2018).

Mukta, Parita. 'Mirabai in Rajasthan'. *Manushi* 50–52, pp. 94–99 (1989).

Pandey, S.M., and Norman Zide. 'Mirabai and Her Contributions to the Bhakti Movement'. *History of Religions* 5, no. 1, pp. 54–73. The University of Chicago Press (1965).

Prasad, Munshi Devi. *Miram Bai ka Jivan Charitra,* ed. Lalit Prasad Shukla. Bangiya Hindi Parishad, Calcutta. (original 1898).

Taft, Frances. 'The Elusive Historical Mirabai: A Note,' in Lawrence A. Babb, Varsha Joshi, and Michael Meister, eds., *Multiple Histories: Culture, and Society in the Study of Rajasthan*. Jaipur: Rawat Publications, 2002, pp. 313–335.

Varghese, Ritu. 'Mirabai in Popular Imagination: Reading Bhakti Canon in Contemporary Context'. *Artha*-Journal of Social Sciences 2020, Vol. 19, No. 2, pp. 67–81.

Websites

https://hindi-kavita.com/SantMeeraBai.php

Acknowledgements

I am grateful to Anupriya for understanding the brief and doing the artwork for this volume with such quiet ease. I owe thanks to Mriga Maithel for her editorial suggestions and input, and to Bidisha Srivastava, my editor at Amaryllis for editing as well as for her capable stewardship in bringing this volume together. And as always, I'm grateful to my agent Smita Khanna and to Jacaranda Literary Agency for having my back.

Also from Amaryllis

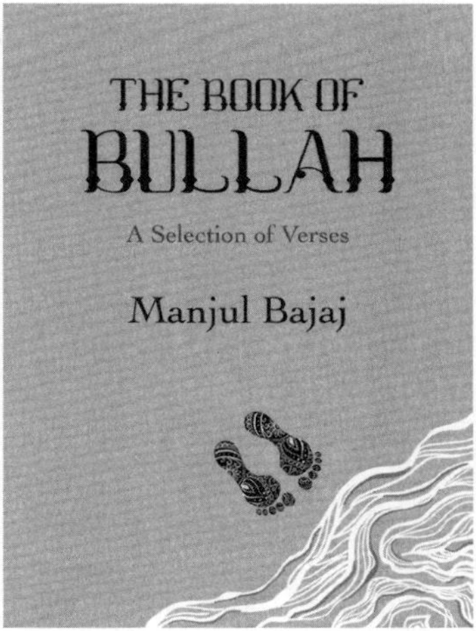

In *The Book of Bullah: A Selection of Verses*, the first book in the Bhakti series, author Manjul Bajaj interprets the imagery and symbols, metaphors and motifs of Bulleh Shah's verses for the modern reader and presents a hundred of his poems in a fresh and lucid English translation.

The Songs of Meera

Manjul Bajaj graduated in Economics followed by masters degrees in Rural Management and Environmental Science. She worked as a development and environment professional for many years before becoming an author. Her debut novel, *Come, Before Evening Falls*, was shortlisted for The Hindu Literary Prize 2010 and her collection of short stories, *Another Man's Wife*, was shortlisted for The Hindu Literary Prize 2013. Her novel *In Search of Heer* was listed for several prizes including the JCB Prize for Literature in 2020. She is also the author of *The Book of Bullah: A Selection of Verses*, and *Elbie's Quest* and *Nargisa's Adventures*, two books for children. Her latest work is *Once Upon a Summer*, a novel. She lives in Goa with her husband.